MW00366367

INSECURITY SYSTEM

About the Lexi Rudnitsky First Book Prize in Poetry

The Lexi Rudnitsky First Book Prize in Poetry is a collaboration between Persea Books and The Lexi Rudnitsky Poetry Project. It sponsors the annual publication of a collection by a woman who has yet to publish a full-length poetry book.

Lexi Rudnitsky (1972–2005) grew up outside of Boston. She studied at Brown University and Columbia University, where she wrote poetry and cultivated a profound relationship with a lineage of women poets that extends from Muriel Rukeyser to Heather McHugh. Her own poems exhibit both a playful love of language and a fierce conscience. Her writing appeared in *The Antioch Review, Columbia: A Journal of Literature and Art, The Nation, The New Yorker, The Paris Review, Pequod*, and *The Western Humanities Review*. In 2004, she won the Milton Kessler Memorial Prize for Poetry from *Harpur Palate*. Lexi died suddenly in 2005, just months after the birth of her first child and the acceptance for publication of her first book of poems, *A Doorless Knocking into Night* (Mid-List Press, 2006). The Lexi Rudnitsky First Book Prize in Poetry was founded to memorialize her and to promote the type of poet and poetry in which she so spiritedly believed.

Previous winners of the Lexi Rudnitsky First Book Prize in Poetry

2018   Valencia Robin, *Ridiculous Light*
2017   Emily Van Kley, *The Cold and the Rust*
2016   Molly McCully Brown,
        The Virginia State Colony for Epileptics and Feebleminded
2015   Kimberly Grey, *The Opposite of Light*
2014   Susannah Nevison, *Teratology*
2013   Leslie Shinn, *Inside Spiders*
2012   Allison Seay, *To See the Queen*
2011   Laura Cronk, *Having Been an Accomplice*
2010   Cynthia Marie Hoffman, *Sightseer*
2009   Alexandra Teague, *Mortal Geography*
2008   Tara Bray, *Mistaken for Song*
2007   Anne Shaw, *Undertow*
2006   Alena Hairston, *The Logan Topographies*

INSECURITY SYSTEM
POEMS
SARA WAINSCOTT

A KAREN & MICHAEL BRAZILLER BOOK

PERSEA BOOKS / NEW YORK

Copyright © 2020 by Sara Wainscott

All rights reserved. No part of this publication may be reproduced or transmitted in any form or by any means, electronic or mechanical, including photocopy, audio recording, or any information storage and retrieval system, without prior permission in writing from the publisher. Request for permission or for information should be addressed to the publisher:

Persea Books, Inc.
90 Broad Street
New York, New York 10004

Library of Congress Cataloging-in-Publication Data

Names: Wainscott, Sara, author.
Title: Insecurity system : poems / Sara Wainscott.
Description: New York : A Karen & Michael Braziller Book / Persea Books, [2020]
    Summary: "Winner of the 2019 Lexi Rudnitsky First Book Prize in Poetry,
    Insecurity System by Sara Wainscott is a wry exploration of memory,
    motherhood, interplanetary time-travel, and the precarious future. Propelled
    by existential longing, these poems cycle between tenderness and rage, desire
    and despair, tracking the intertwined anxieties of making a living and making
    a life"—Provided by publisher.

Identifiers: LCCN 2019044338 | ISBN 9780892555048 (paperback)
Subjects: LCGFT: Poetry.
Classification: LCC PS3623.A35626 I57 2020 | DDC 811/.6—dc23
LC record available at https://lccn.loc.gov/2019044338

Book design and composition by Rita Lascaro
Typeset in Palatino
Manufactured in the United States of America. Printed on acid-free paper.

Contents

Know this in your heart [

  ] would free me from all my worries

Sappho (translated by Jim Powell)

INSECURITY SYSTEM

SPACESHIP

Cut buds bloom awhile in a water glass
and demonstrate the perfect grace

that comes with dying. What am I saying?
I am saying that I love to be alive,

but love's a violent feeling. I'm powerless
beside the honey bees who have no cares

but industry. Kindness is important work
but I am weak. I'm not the woman

I thought I'd be. What kind of heaven
is available only to the dead?

If I were a clover in the lawn I'd have more sway
with myself, I'd tender more to gentleness.

In another life I walk a mile to the train
past a pair of red lions offering their fangs.

Red lions holding out for a better offer
on their single-family home.
After three hundred days, a little waiting
makes the money sweeter
when they eat it.
My muscles brace my arms
on the train like it's a basketball game
and I'm boxing out.

I'm heading home to display
a bowl of apples, because still life
lends plain old shit a sense of perfection.
The lions are statues, but I think of them as people,

sweet on each other pointlessly,
standing up as if there were no seasons.

In the season of withstanding,
memory fails the test. *Blah-blah* o'clock

the robin rocks. The poets say
that *while ye may*
rosebuds exist for gathering.
Maybe a mind's locationless, and then
to be is clearly *not.*

I am tired of minding for those who do not mind.
Tiredness is not much reason to give up.

There is no rightness like a rose.
Tipped into a hole, the ailing brain
shoots the family marbles.
Circles the drain.

Cue the rage of any reasonable person.

A person doesn't need a reason
to build a flying saucer on her *own damn property*:
people have to be allowed some space

to figure out the limits of their understanding.
I think it's normal to be terrified
of losing it

—but I should probably relax.
The birds in the sky belong in the sky
and I belong

to you. In a perfect world I would
belong to myself.

Anything else is loss. To make a bird
you have to break some eggs. Throw yourself

to the sky and see what comes down.

The sky does not come down for me,
though I have cried for it to meet me at the lake.

The ice has ragged edges like a pinhole photo.
Rilke's panther hides a picture in its heart.

When I'm reading books or circling words in student work
a paragraph is a fence and *a fence is a neighbor.*

One electrifies, one lies torn apart for weeks.
Even if you don't capture it, a word is not a wild animal.

A mind can be a fence, a code punched
into a worn keypad or cracked, an insecurity system.

A child's bed with clip-on sides, just high enough
to keep her there, little lamb waiting to be counted.

The sky does not come down.
The pain of waking seels the eye in sleep.

Seals sleep behind a pane
plump and unwild

I dream the blade
unbuttons their red suits

in the arctic salt they shiver
calling to the pups

falling into the upright void
of a drowned crescent

then the womb
swells my other creature

thrashing the sheets and I turn
down a country road

where preachers park their traveling shows
and kids vanish into the field

The kids ride bikes into the field
and I'm watching a rape scene

and the kids pretend
to lock each other up like cops

and I'm a silent movie queen
posing for a photo with my shoulders curled

inside an egg back when
I spared a thought for other people

and I'm calling them to wash for dinner
and they belong to me

and I cry like a swan into the field
because I *can't remember anything but longing*

and how callous I can be to close
the door and keep my comforts for myself

I used to keep my problems to myself
but now I have a therapist who says
you must be open to the world.
Opening up makes me feel gut-shot
but expert advice is expensive
so I take it. I say sometimes the sea is more
than I pictured as a landlocked kid
—it is a page that fills but cannot fill.
I say the men are hammering the roof.
I say Mars is a speck of boiled blood
and the moon seems like a real cool place
to have a hysterectomy. I say
I hope the moon takes my insurance.
I say once ants get in they stay all summer.

It slays me in summer
how a flowerbed of bees can zip
a building's features. Waiting makes me
calm but angry. A brass cannon
blazes in a sunny square.

Summertime and the easy
force of nail guns nailing across the alley
when I come home to you. Some of it
I'm making up. Some seasons
hadn't had a roof.

Men fielding headlights between the lanes
have bright new vests. Easy

to notice · sturdy things · lilies.
Alive and permissive as I'd love to be.

to be the page that fills but cannot fill to be the page that
fills but cannot fill to be the page that fills but cannot fill to be the
page that fills but cannot fill to be the page that fills but cannot fill
to be the page that fills but cannot fill to be the page that fills but
cannot fill to be the page that fills but cannot fill to be the page that
fills but cannot fill to be the page that fills but cannot fill to be the
page that fills but cannot fill to be the page that fills but cannot fill
to be the page that fills but cannot fill to be the page that fills but
cannot fill to be the page that fills but cannot fill to be the page that
fills but cannot fill to be the page that fills but cannot fill to be the
page that fills but cannot fill to be the page that fills but cannot fill
to be the page that fills but cannot fill to be the page that fills but
cannot fill to be the page that fills but cannot fill to be the page that
fills but cannot fill to be the page that fills but cannot fill

Pills and rage, I reply when people say
I'm looking well these days.
The rosebush I love best
grows on the roadside boulevard.
Most of the time, I wouldn't hurt a flea.
I wouldn't pluck a rose that didn't belong to me.
I take pictures on my phone, but they don't
show the lived experience of roses.
Rosebushes don't belong to anyone,
I think, yet do not touch.
For roses I feel a reverence
usually reserved for the dead. The dead
don't like me much—they're sick of flowers.
Upon the pikes the pink heads glower.

Heads grow among the spikes

· rows of roses · fake like faux

roses · pink and nude · Fox News

logo burned into the TV screen ·

ride bikes into the field · read

books to ride the planets · *you*

have to be this tall · the spires pin

a cloud · puffed up the face-

down body floated · the rows

rise exactly so · below the oak

the spaceship swings · follow

the lines like life support · wires

spun between the pines

· *contrails* and *red buttons*

A button controls them runs them
through the photocopier these smashed faces
printed as though on a windshield
where doomed bugs hit

There's hundreds of them
papering a horror movie farmhouse
They keep saying it can't be real

bugs are not the form they like
but damn if that's not what they're folded into
tucked between the serrated branches
of a basement's foil-cased ducts

They are singing of the air
oh many of them are singing
of the air they are

In cold air the kids are coughing,
catapulting the particles
which collaborate

to form colonies of goo.
When they are not
on the yellow bus to school

their boots stay home too.
Barefoot on the stair they rule.

Hear how the heart
struggles against its muscle—
even in the hush

between the footfalls,
the meadow inside the snow
and the grubs inside the meadow.

The cat rubs her shadow
across the curtain,
translating the lambent air
to limbs.

Spirited so,
we make a home.
We plot our obsolescence
and hatch our tallies.

Pollen drifts one place or another.
Fish float to the moon.
Horses flick their lively legs
as we did,

as children do,
showing off their cuts.

FLOWERISH

A moth flits across the screen
like a starlet searching out a searing kiss,
like I will have my heart's desire
even if my lights get snuffed.

Paste-colored clouds puff.
I powder up, I stuff
my mouth with marshmallows.
Surely I deserve a treat
even if I must take it lying down

in grass so stiff my thighs prickle.
Getting nowhere feels sweet and human
but I hit the bricks because it's good to get out.
A streetlight flickers in the asphalt oil slicks,
wet and lively as a rainbow trout.

Lovely as a rainbow trout I imagine
words you use to compliment my looks,
though you neglect to. *Thou art a rose*
you also neglect to use, though surely you mean to
floralize me, for *I art.*

People who read poems know a rose
is how the poet drags in genitalia.
Let me save some trouble—I have it,
a worn-out beauty of a cunt,
folded, tanned, and stitched up
tighter than a taxidermy cat.
Of course I love you,

for love admires its reflection. My next life:
brine collecting in a mollusk's shell.

The shine of a mollusk's shell
is a living anyone can earn,
though I prefer the richer temptations
of regular pay. Other people I mistake
for sculptures. Existence must be pristine

when living's not a bother.
Everywhere waiting is expected
I take a book, which doesn't bother anybody.
Surgeons plant an ear inside an artist's arm,
though listening isn't always an embrace.

My head has a factory face and inside
a handsome white man screams into a microphone
about salacious things that can result
when girls sit in parked cars.

When girls sit in parked cars
they turn to fish. The breath gets heavy.
Soft! what man through yonder window

shows his cock on a public bus?
A clown car generates another clown, and fear
spit-shines the dime.

Looks are subject to other people's faces
if other people can be trusted.
Other people I despise

because self-loathing
extends to anyone who appears to find
the world a normal place to live.

The breath gets heavy.
It's easy to pretend to be asleep.

Sleep is the pretense of ease.
Sleep aggravates the cash flow problem.
I quit the *real job*s and keep the stupid ones
because of my distaste for work.
Cheekbones earn sweet talk and they deserve it.

Before a party I slap my face
to help me seem to flourish. Flowerish
I attend a party, but then of course
I must attend a party. A portrait of a princess
is a lost da Vinci is a knock-off grocery girl.

Occasion imposes on me to rise.
I'm as sensitive as a poet, as a rose
languishing in a photograph
of Jacqueline Onassis.

O Jackie! hear my sorrow.
A summary in flowers of my feelings
could overflow a field. Out for a breakfast
of cinnamon toast I

overflow again. All I do of late is flow.
I weep for the racehorses
whose cropped hides remind me
my shortcomings know

no such penance. I sob in crowds.
What's bone is bone.
The rarest rose cannot be found.

Petals pressed, and then more pressure.
Bowels evacuated during labor.
Pairs of legs flung rowdily around.

Around the flowering pears
drones inspect the softest spots.

Mars Needs Babies. The youngest
gets the needle in her thigh.

The money went someplace
and the muscles heaved, pulling back

the sleeves to reach the deeper pocket.
A notice from the tax man

stuck up with refrigerator magnets.
The things I'll have to do.

Kittens in a pet shop window
I please to raise on milk at home.

Vein-blue milk a violet scratch
welling up a rose-red dew.

Swelling up as roses do
on Mars my bedroom
dead west faces down each day's
phlegmatic prisms on the wall.

Then to work I leave the dwelling
lest I would keep home

and settle. Well would I
wide-eyed master
complex novel tasks just as bees
learn to map the human face.

Dead cool like Freddy Mercury
infrared goggles filtering the room.
Light hearts under martial law, light hearts
fooling at the airlock doors.

I lock the door and leave for work.

Sky like black pools

on the moon. Sea of Tranquility.

Sea of Fertility.

Sea of Crises. Sea of Nectar. Sea of Clouds.

Questions and questions

and checklists of possible answers.

Sea of Dementia. Sea of Depression.

Sea of School Bus. Sea of Laundry.

Headlights like globes

of shaken glycerin and glitter.

The roads have been erased by snow

which goes to show

the illusion of having options.

Clouds are optical illusions.
Crowding out the other organs
is the corollary of decision.

As if to know my mind I must
invent pathologies,
as if there were a base I might return to,
a brick ranch house on a busy thoroughfare

where in the fall the roses blow,
scattering messy
peach matter, strewing

the road with red.
Flowers are devices of the dead.
Posies unpocketed. Masses of the opiate, perhaps.
Little birds attacking a hawk.

Birds attack a little town—on and on
the children warble. In the final scene, the survivors
drive away. Why do they save the lovebirds?

Bones show up everywhere
in poems. I must make space for them: [
                                        ].

I must try to have sex
dreams in which I contribute more vigorously.
Clouds illustrate

the air's colossal control. I'd like
that wouldn't I—? O Death, *u won't shut up.*

A cage gets cozy, but
even in the final scene
it's good to feel the itch to sing.

It's great to feel rich and not be
taken to collections.

Galleries leave wall space between exhibits
to show how effortless
is worth.

In my self portrait
a bitch whelps on a nest of bills.

In bed I turn aside though I am willing
to turn back. Over a basket
spill the silver innards. Over the edge.

Sharp stroke. My nape. Once and quick. The heart
can not get out. A ruby we recline.

Milk and honey. Will I will. My gold mine!
my livid planet! Breaking unto thee.

Breakfast on a silver platter
in the fashion of a fairy-princess tale,
then down the beach path the tourists scramble
hauling shovels and buckets and babies.
Far in front, the kids have nearly reached the sky.
Flannel clouds disperse the gray.

The kids walk out on the mud flats
far away where sand sucks their ankles,
but they make it back to the mothers tearing
string cheese sleeves. We are seals now
they call between themselves
and it is true. Their mothers step into

black SUVs and fly away home, and the seals
look out at the sea, not ready to try.

Leaking out · not ready to see this · because if I am a *dumb bitch*
then it's my job to tell myself · when I am sitting in a blue skirt
by water · water takes on the sky's circumstances · if I am a horse
for work I want to work · if I am a horse for show I want to show
beautifully · water as sallow as yellow glass · and my wrist hurts
because I wrote a note to a mother because her boy swallowed
a lake · because the current pulled him back · if he can not get out
I can not get out · little fishes moving back and forth in a glass ·
because wrongly I would rather be quiet than wrong · because
given the circumstances I make allowance · because *here you are
having fun and your brother lays there dying* · if I am a horse ·
if I am a boy · if the amount of matter is always exactly the same ·
I show my stomach to a doctor · water the color of worn money ·
water the color of the bucket's bottom · water the color of olives

Watercolor roses

they painted like pink

vitamins crushed up

swirled in the milk cup

my son and my daughter

wait like goblins wait

for their next birthdays

for the solid proof they

lay their goblin paws

on the cabbage of my belly

scarred and clawed

full of motion like a tank

of frilled moon jellies or

a tank rolling across a green

FUTURE CITIES

There's no way this can end well,
I tell the movie people who are laughing
in relief at what seems to be unfounded fear.
Someone else is always watching.
They won't get one word out.

My zebra panties in the wash again.
Obligation ≠ invitation.
Sentences become drawn-out affairs
but I am doing what I can
to answer one word every day.

Enormous pinecones club the lawn.
A child creeps into a cave.

I levitate at will and would
come home were home my name for it.

Come *home,* the name for it
unfixed and yet
embedded. A rose was me
in a past go-round and gave up too.
Trick a brain to sleep

with computerized renditions of lake sounds,
barf roses into everything,
sponge every crevice of a mouth.
If I wanted to, I could.
I could come into the house

because I am not chained without.
I am pulled into a memory

of a modest bedroom
preserved exactly as my last self left it.

The last bone left is served
to dogs. The gods ate first.

Clouds at morning. Loud mornings.
Out-loud mourning. The last
tune left. I zip my mouth,

I button it. My lips are sealed, my lips
are leased. I'm writing you a letter.
I'm writing you. I'm writing.

And so the days last.
We write to transform, I say
out loud at the front of a classroom.

But we abide. You are a cloud
and I am another cloud, and writing this
perpetuates the going on.

I'm going on and on
about the roses.

I want to be laughing in a hallway
with you. In a painting
a woman wore a sea monster in her hair.

This is how lovely
I think laughter could be.

This is how distant. People calling
to each other. The babies
wrapped in cotton fluff.

What is distance when there is no space?
Someone ought to shut me up.

Quite likely the clouds feel no sense
of obligation to the sky.

Sky towers deep and mineral.

Papers bending through the weeds.

The heavy morning sleep balloon.

One more day, like insects.

The beverage stations of the office maze.

The gnat cloud cortex.

The bright spots of spacecraft overhead.

The moonlike moon, not even metal.

Little mouth to eat the mush.

The ancient engorgement.

Back and forth, cars averaging their movements.

Perfectly squared table and chairs.

What choice but turning back the clock:

The sun requesting payment.

A question's frame
projects a version of the future

in the asking. A rocket
pressed into a penny

illustrates the atom's vaster scale.
What chasm is wonder.

When I am here, I sleep
in future cities

where intermittent diodes
strung among the grafted plants

alternate their green displays,
where a pair of nervous swans

flaps on a retention pond
like hands spreading out a cloth.

A band of moonlight spreads
across the bedroom windowpane,
thin and clear as vinegar.

Fish live on the moon and swim
by night, bright milk-eyes
who lip the ovaries.

In my next life I will love you better.
I will live on Mars and tend
the giant red roses. And where

will you be, and where our boy?

Silence responds to silence.
I don't feel like a mother any more.
The moon slivers to a needle
sewing stars into a river.

Drive the car into a river
because you
control the radio.
The stars keep playing the same old song.
Quail, quail, throw yourself into the sea.

What do you think
of French cuffs if it's your shirt
on me? There's more
of me where I come from.
A vitrine of seashells decorates a quiet room.

Your heart should be a private thing,
you animal. What decadence

to make a show of it, to allow the air
every ministration.

Vermin in the station and garbage fires
and spiders chewing through the walls.
Pink plastic roses. Into the tunnels

artists haul their spray cans, making
thunder when they shake them,
cellophane stripped from a bouquet

or platelets sloshing in the human heart.
Lay down your money and you play your part.
Picket fences follow a gravel path
into a neighborhood bordered by arterials

and artificial ponds. Ranch dressing
on the french fries and the salads.
Teach a man to fish, the tax man laughs,
and success becomes a dirty subject.

The subjectivity of success
riles up the class I should be teaching.

The gladdest heart's a waste
if all you need is hustle.

It's tough to think the moon's
a flake, a swear-licked soap cake,

a person who pretends it's fine
you're fucking other people.

It takes guts to get ahead, they say.
A thesis statement sets a limit.

Some governments shoot poems
into space, some shoot poets.

For fewer but more perfect blooms,
experts say to prune the buds.

Say
Boss
I'm
starvin
too
it's
dark
down
here
I'm
dyin
for
some
action

Dying is an action. Like petals
flung, you flatten out across a posh avenue,
blow your brains into a hotel lobby where one time

as a child you dreamed yourself into the picture
of a horse roll-eyed in a wheat field,
boy and girl a-following.

Ink arranges on the page as blots
inside itself. You do

not do. Dying is inaction,
and there's time enough for that.
There's a billion videos on YouTube: Lana Del Rey,
octopus babies hiccup through a cave,

cyborgs crimp the flesh-suits. *Vanish the night,*
the gray stars, the rosy rooster wails.

Stars like gray whales on the roof.
In our bed I red-cheeked rest,

pigeonholed, tilted rose.
The sky's a box of diamond light

projecting into space our copulations.
Probably the planets mock us.

Why say these things to you?
Why say anything? I don't consent

to feeling closeness. There are many
ways to get warm. I wake

and rest my skull against the wall.
Spring is coming with its brand new colors.

The words for everything. Those very things.
Motes of dust that travel into space.

The space you held is traced in dust.
Waves control the mind's living states.
The world's so brutal it's absurd.

I find your handwriting in books,
I read the lines you marked.
For bliss, as thou hast part, to me is bliss.

Permeating violet blue.
Impermanence. What happened to you

happened, you made certain of it, even if
you had to write it down.
The brain is porous as a coral reef.

The brain is dead, which is to say
bleached or bludgeoned or far from home.
Bowl of berries. Big blue moon.

Buried on the moon
in other lives I left behind
for someone else some trace. I rose,

I rise. Irises,
but to call them blood-blue is too burlesque.
Most of me I have not left
and in this way scale back
as though anything

will keep me from the air's infinite arcs,
as though I could exist here
or would wish to.

The moon's an embryonic place.
What's left I mean to thrust away
but there is no *away*.

THE SUPERNATURAL VIOLET BLUES

We come back ahead of *time*
and smash the 4th dimension.

Reverse the ship so fast we pass
ourselves on the approach

and infinitely faster yet
we zap the mountaintop.

We sleep thinly in corolla-cover
near the locked atomic clocks,

we sleep our other selves.
Our heartbeats can't go back

but every moment
gain a moment, leading

adjacent lives
between which all time slips.

I punch my time slip after my shift
and walk to the beach

where waves chop, sharp and even,
a knife set in a block.

Ants defend their pyramids of sand.
The future is happening, but not

the way I swore.
I wanted to be a mother

more than I wanted to be myself.
I would rather not regret this.

A dog shits and turns to kick the sand,
then races into a receding wave.

The lake holds back the landscape,
the idle crowd, the clouds on which the cherubs perch.

idyll before the clouds come down
        before the light turns green
                before the cicadas shrill again

in bodies the blood
        goes out to sea
                the heart a tireless apology

        did you read that now we have an extra moon

between two points the worms
        move openly
                within their element

a knife beneath the bed will cut the pain in two
                        and the drugs will whet the knife

        sunbeams lavishing our paradise
with gentle punishment

Push me very gently
into oncoming traffic

is a dream-thing I talk you into.
I, a jam sandwich,

tuck raspberries in my hair.
Pearl ring rolls right off

the dresser. It's impossible
to imagine how I

could deserve you.
Your hands smell of grease

and grass, the consequence
of weekend mornings.

I know a good thing when I see it
and maybe I get busy.

I get a business card
from a man looking to *have a coffee,*
trade some poems.

Gene Kelly holding out a red rose
in *An American in Paris* gives me the razzle-dazzle.
Like a sunflower

I'm pulled down by the weight
of my own head. I thought
by now I'd live on Mars. *Have a coffee,*

kill myself? turns out not to be a thing
Camus said, but it reminds me of Seattle
when I lived there nearly lakeside

in a fresh century, below a sappy pine tree, with
a boy and his dog for my friends, and nothing more.

A boy and a dog frenzied on a green.
The time involved changes cake's shape,
participating heat does factor.

A boy up in the night to vomit.
That morning at the zoo-show a pony
let him drag a curry comb along her flank.

On the album cover, two men spread
their limbs across a vinyl sofa. A figurine
of a woman and her greyhounds

gives a room an elegance, an air of chintz.
The dogs thrust their slim muzzles
against her china skirts. People

underwater on a house. People reading
about the lives of martyrs.

To live on Mars and have
a bedroom there does not come true.

How to look out on palm trees from a balcony
without wanting to leap into violet blue?

How transparent the stars appear.
How obdurate their want.

Why should roses have to mean?
Making meaning leaves out far too much.

And death, which leaves out meaning.
I am not equipped for this.

From the highest corner
a harlequin is clinging to the moon.

Ophelia sings and someone's hands
mold the lyrics into signs.

Told the lyre: how the head sighs
throws a wild concert
rushing riverdown
to rejoin the fragments
the blood-eaters
eat what they can reach

they the mosquitoes
and they the witnesses

of the evening's main event
sing the body severed yet
the supernatural violet blues
do not relent
they are the spiral holding up the sky
the scarab in the supplicant's ear

Scars grow supple as they heal,
but words fill up with violet blue

and violet blue fills up the words
and the words refuse

to empty out or overturn. You push
more gently than is possible to do with hands

until even tenderness feels vicious.
Two things can be just alike

but it's a mistake to think that you can tell.
You leave the house, come home.

Only you can know. Inside the house
the supernatural violet blue

opens up your gut to eat the fat,
then glues it back as barren as a blackout.

Blackouts are *the practice*
of collectively minimizing outdoor light
but mainly a test to make sure people obey.
Deliberate silence
sometimes is anodyne,
sometimes suppression.
Roses are how I understand
individual excellence as an act of community.
We *don't want trouble*. Sit down, *sit down*.
A little moonlight can kill a man.
A man followed me today to where I'd left my car.
The skyline's piled syringes are the palaces of empire
and while these structures stand, some people
still enjoy freedom of passage.

Free to pass among the pleasure domes · along
the rank river · reminds me Mr. Sad Face lives

on the bank or at it · but the red and purple horses
look melancholy too · *their legs got stuck there* · I am free

to pull my own weight through the fog's weight · stuck
at work till 1 AM · can't eat a whole melon · it's natural

to push this way · he *don't want to play games* · horses
along the river take the trails like tourists · the dew

I taste in honeydew is seasonal · the verdant bank
sounds vaginal · listen, horses make sick lovers

· I'm a thought, a pansy · but they do not pansy me
a lick · natural to fog awake at 1 AM · *I'll take you in*

to rob the bank · laugh about all kinds of money ·
tear my papers · jerk it in the over-honeyed hayfield

In the fields, bees jerk between the one-eyed flowers,
shaking gold dust from their jackets
and regurgitating

sweets to feed their queen. White flowers
and pink flowers, and in the crotches
the filamentary

clouds weighted
from within by worms.

Bette Davis couldn't be happy
on a pleasure cruise in love with a married man
so she pinned a white camellia to her blouse, o saint

of sexual incompetents meant to live alone—
and now the obligatory birds appear
to cram their lungs with light.

Lighten up! go the hot night guns
as they spray exploding flowers above a public schoolyard,
showing the crowd how fire-power is a form of splendor.
Summertime and the living is about the same
for those who all year have it good.

I haven't got a perfect heart, but I'm pretty happy
when it forgets to beat me shitless.
I'm okay, I say, which means the world
can't take anything I don't acknowledge.
A heart shouldn't take on too much

but what could ever really be enough?
Buttercups go off without a bang, but I can't
get off without one. When I'm hot at night, I picture
the tax man slowly taking back my blanket.

The mind goes blank, black and low,
pulled into the gravity
of a collapsing star.
Rose, thou art sick,
and *lay me down,* and *here*
I stay. Here the kids are leaping
from the roof, here the all-night bonfires
are sending fallen leaves to hell.

Future to future and past to past.
The law exists against forgetting.
I will get what I pay for
and then I must continue making payments.
The tax man tallies up the petals
in a secret second bedroom.

One second in a room
        on Mars · one hour

                and wormholes and strangers
      must transport me

to when last we spoke together
      · or last will speak · or speak at last

     clock resets · the moon
         chalks up another zero

   there's no way this can end

   arriving the same
      and pursuing again

               cut buds bloom
      awhile in a water glass

and then the dead come back

Notes

[In the season of withstanding] is in conversation with, and borrows language from, Robert Herrick's poem "To the Virgins, to Make Much of Time" and from *Hamlet*. The poem also misremembers Bobby Day's song "Rockin' Robin" as a mashup with Bill Haley's "Rock Around the Clock."

[The sky does not come down for me] references Sherman Alexie's essay "Superman and Me" and Robert Frost's poem "Mending Wall."

[The kids ride bikes into the field] borrows a line from Jim Powell's translation of "The Anectoria Poem" which appears in *The Poetry of Sappho*.

[The shine of a mollusk's shell] references the artist Stelarc's "extra ear" project (2007).

[Sleep is the pretense of ease] references "La Bella Principessa," a controversial drawing attributed to either Leonardo da Vinci or British art forger Shaun Greenhalgh, as reported in the December 4, 2015 *New York Times* article "An Art World Mystery Worthy of Leonardo."

[I lock the doors and leave for work] references "Section 1: The lunar seas," an online supplement to the documentary serial *The Sky at Night*, which appears on *BBC 4*.

[Sky towers deep and mineral] reimagines a line from Joseph Ceravolo's poem "The Rocket," which appears in the collection *Millenium Dust*.

[Drive the car into a river] references the myth of Asteria.

[Vermin in the station and garbage fires] borrows a line from Bruce Springsteen's song "Hungry Heart," from the album *The River*.

[Say] is after and for Bruce Springsteen, and it borrows language from his song "Dancin' In the Dark," from the album *Born In The USA*.

[Dying is an action] reimagines language from Giacomo Puccini's "Nessun Dorma," which appears in the opera *Turandot*, as translated anonymously on Wikipedia.

[The space you held is traced in dust] borrows line 879 from Book 9 of Milton's *Paradise Lost*.

[Buried on the moon] considers a quotation from Barry Commoner's book *The Closing Circle*.

[An idyll before the clouds come down] references the June 27, 2016 article "NASA Discovered a "Mini" Moon Orbiting Earth," which appears on the website *The Science Explorer*.

[Blackouts are the practice] borrows language from the Wikipedia entry "Blackout (wartime)."

[In the fields, bees jerk between the one-eyed flowers] references the film *Now, Voyager*.

[Lighten up, go the hot night guns] borrows language from George Gershwin's song "Summertime."

[The mind goes blank, black and low] references William Blake's poem "The Sick Rose," a traditional children's prayer, and a story recounted in L.M. Montgomery's novel *Emily of New Moon*.

Acknowledgments

Publications in which these poems, some in earlier versions, have appeared:

"[Birds attack a little town—on and on]," "[It's great to feel rich]," and "[Leaking out • not ready to see this • because if I am a *dumb bitch*] in *Ghost Ocean*; "[Breakfast on a silver platter]" and "[There's no way this can end well]" in *Grimoire*; "[The subjectivity of success]," "[Cut buds bloom awhile in a water glass]," "[Red lions holding out for a better offer]," "[In the season of withstanding]," and "[A person doesn't need a reason] in *The Collapsar*; "[I'm going on and on]" and "[Drive the car into a river]" in *The Journal*; "[*Lovely as a rainbow trout* I imagine]," "[The shine of a mollusk's shell]," "[When girls sit in parked cars]," "[Sleep is the pretense of ease]," "[O Jackie! hear my sorrow]," "[Around the flowering pears]," "[Swelling up as roses do]," and "[I lock the doors and leave]" in *The Journal Petra*. Thanks to the editors.

An earlier version of "[The sky does not come down for me]" is featured in the February 14, 2017 episode of the poetry podcast *Make[No]Bones*. Thanks to Toby Altman and Emily Barton-Altman.

Thanks to Karen and Michael Braziller, the Lexi Rudnitsky family, and Gabe Fried for guidance and support.

Thanks to Jennifer Nelson, Jessica Johnson, Kevin Edwards, Meredith Lewis, Sonia Greenfield, Megan Snyder-Camp, Philip Sorenson, Olivia Cronk, Amanda Marbais, Ian McCarty, and Nathan Hoks for camaraderie and encouragement and truth.

Thanks and deep gratitude to my teachers, Jack Hibbard, Steve

Klepetar, Bill Meissner, James Anderson, Jack Wang, Colleen McElroy, Linda Bierds, Heather McHugh, and Rick Kenney for generosity and counsel, and with particular thanks to Tim Hall for believing this book was inevitable.

Thanks to my parents and family for love and security, and especially to Egon, Errol, and Helen, who helped me be in several places at once: this book is for you.